Marion Delana Daniel McConnell

Sheaves of Song

Marion Delana Daniel McConnell

Sheaves of Song

ISBN/EAN: 9783337181420

Printed in Europe, USA, Canada, Australia, Japan

Cover: Foto ©Thomas Meinert / pixelio.de

More available books at **www.hansebooks.com**

SHEAVES OF SONG

BY

MARION DELANA DANIEL

BUFFALO
THE PETER PAUL BOOK COMPANY
1895

TO MY MOTHER.

CONTENTS.

NATURE.

LIFE.

CONTENTS.

LOVE.

HEAVEN.

NATURE

NATURE.

"THE world a book," God's testament,
    A poem of the soul,
Writ in the azure firmament
    On purple parchment scroll.

The stars His thoughts, inscribed in gold,
    The silence chants His speech ;
The secrets of His page unfold
    Themselves in Nature's reach ;

The moon, the sun, their incense raise,
    Adoring Nature's King;
The rocks His sermons, and for praise
    " The stars together sing;"

The sea, the sky, the smiling flowers,
    Evangels of His art,
And e'en these human hearts of ours
    Portray the Writer's Heart.

NATURE'S MUSIC.

UPON the stones,
        Sweet organs in their reach,
The water-sprites, upon the beach,
Play Nature's thought and Poet's speech
        In music tones.

In tender touch,
Deep, regular and full of tone,
Upon the keys of jutting stone,
The chords of Nature, one by one,
        Their echoes couch.

Sometimes in beat
Of dashing spray, she plays the part
Of passion-note, of bounding heart;
Then sings her soul with slower start,
        In minors sweet.

For viol strings,
The whispering winds she deftly takes,
And breathing low sweet tremors, wakes
Pathetic pleading, passion-breaks,
        On music wings.

Till through the still
Of woodland vistas, if you list,
You catch the mystic music mist
By golden light and zephyrs kiss't,—
A breathing thrill !

But sweetest tone
That Nature's music ever swells,
She murmurs to the ocean shells
In echoed chords, like chiming bells,
The deep sea's moan.

TO MANCHESTER.

ON the bosom of thy calmness, bear me, Rustic
Dove of rest,
To the deep and whispering shadows, 'neath some
quiet, sunny crest;

Lead me from the toil and tumult of the city's
clang and din
To the still and shady woodlands where stray sunbeams flicker in;

To the cool and limpid waters strolling past a
mossy glade,
Where the cow-slips and the daisies wander through
the sylvan shade;

Bear me to the rocky ledges, to a fern-draped
brooklet's brink,
Where the blushing rustic roses bend their rosy lips
to drink;

Where the pine and scented cedars kiss the air
with fragrant breath,
Where the weeping willows murmur o'er the early
blossom's death;

Waft me down the willow beaches, where the frog
    floats in his barge,
Drums to nightingale's andantes on the moon-lit
    water's marge.

THE BROKEN WING.

A LITTLE bird, as blithe and gay
        As ever made the woodlands ring,
Fell from his sky one fateful day,
    And broke his wing.
So piteously he fluttered there,
    Upon the low and barren ground,
While all his mates, on wing in air,
    He, earthward bound.

All mute with pain and grief he lay,
    Deep listening to their distant song,
Until the shadows 'cross his way
    Grew gray and long.
No more he'd rise on soaring wing
    In freedom towards the smiling sky ;
But might he tune his throat to sing
    New melody ?

So, in his song of chastened trill,
    He poured his heart of memory ;
His soul in cry in outward thrill
    Of harmony.

Till through the woods no song is heard,
   No wingèd bird will ever sing
Like to the sweetness of the bird
   With broken wing !

SUNSHINE AND RIVER.

RIPPLING, running, roguish river,
　　Dimpling, dancing down the tide,
Waltzing with a queenly quiver,
　　Happy as the hours glide.

Sunshine wooed thee, won thee, wed thee,
　　Wary, winding, witching wave,
Long he lingered, laughing, loving,
　　In thy limped, lovely lave.

Winged, winning, wilesome wooer,
　　Braver, bolder in his bliss,
Bore thee, blushing, on his bosom,
　　Kissed thee with his kingly kiss.

Then he queried, quarreled, quivered,
　　Chid thee with a cunning chide,
Till thou promised, pretty prattler,
　　To become his beauteous bride.

Now he sparkles, spangles, splashes,
　　All thy bed a brilliant beam,
Wreathing every ripple, ruffle,
　　In a gliding, golden gleam.

TO A WILD ROSE.

ONE day Cupid donned his armor, golden bow
    and silver wings —
Wilesome weapons for his music—'cross a maiden's
    viol strings.

He would shyly touch and tune them with his golden
    bow of love,
Tremor softly cross the fibres till a music motion
    move,

Fill her ear with silver sounding of a timid, thrill-
    ing strain,
Throb his dart in piercing sweetness through her
    heart with tender pain.

      *   *   *   *

Past a garden, fair and blooming where the maiden-
    roses wait,
Some half-budding into blossom, some half-shat-
    tered, blooming late,

Fleets the shining wingèd Cupid to a woodland's
    shady delves,
Where the fairy forest flowers blossom shy as spirit
    elves,

Near a folded bud of beauty, with a dewdrop on her
    cheek,
With her petals scarcely parted — lips asmile — too
    shy to speak,

Nearer steals this wary wooer, with a rosy, roguish
    rush,
Kisses part the dew-wet petals, warms the wild
    rose with Love's blush.

THE SENSITIVE PLANT.

ON a pathway, sheltered, lonely, sensitive and
    shy she dwelt,
Pent within her burdened bosom all the tenderness
    she felt.

Fairly fashioned, fond and fragrant, pinkly blushing
    into bloom,
Sensitive this plant — too modest — hid her heart
    within a tomb.

If a friend or pleading lover even touched her fin-
    ger tips,
Instantly she'd droop and quiver, close her eyelids
    and her lips.

Faintest footfall, touch or notice seemed to shatter
    all her nerve,
Till by-passers left off coming, left her in her shy
    reserve.

E'en her sisters, aunts and cousins, cowslips, daisies
    of the glade
Shun her, gossip of her shyness, call her by her
    name — "Old Maid."

OAK AND IVY.

STAUNCH and strong in manly beauty, grew a
    lord in Forest Glen ;
King encrowned among his comrades, distant, true
    his lofty ken.

Proud his great, distended branches, sheltering shade
    to forest flowers,
Courted by the graceful zephyrs, sunshine smiles
    and April showers.

Unperturbed, majestic, tender, giving shelter, shade, .
    outspread
To the maiden ferns and roses — which fair blossom
    will he wed ?

      *   *   *   *

See the Primrose, pale and sallow, jealous of the
    blushing bloom
Of her younger Wild-rose sister ; see the Blue-
    bell's face agloom !

See the Violets shyly drooping, veiling meek their
    dew-dimmed eyes
Just behind the maiden mosses ; see the Ivy's mute
    surprise.

Humbler than the fern and mosses, crouching lowly
    on the ground ;
Void of fragrance or attraction, dark and green and
    earthward bound.

Ah ! the stately Oak divines her — all her tender-
    ness and trust —
Twines her clinging arms around him, lifts her
    face from out the dust;

Knows her constant, loyal duty, brave capacity to
    rise,
If but smiled on, loved and cherished — knows her
    beauty never dies.

Ah ! he loves her, lifts, inspires — and she finds in
    him her life,
Beautified and beautifying — Sir Oak's loyal Ivy
    wife !

LILIES.

WE read of thee in sacred story,
    Reflections of God's face,
Not ";Solomon arrayed in glory,"
    Could match thy peerless grace.

White-robed and fair in purity,
    With half-hid golden heart.
Enshrined in virgin sanctity,
    Sweet emblems of God's art !

PASSION SONG.

" FOREVER, forever," she passionate sighed,
　　"'Mid posies of poppies my heart would
　　　　abide,
Where drifting and dreaming, sweet senses to steep,
In crimson and scarlet and fancies of sleep.

" Forever, forever, these colors I choose,
The deep red of passion—the golden effuse
Of yellow's effulgence, of all the gay gleams
That dazzle and dance in ecstasy's dreams.

" Forever, forever," ecstatic she cried,
To rushes of water, of torrent and tide
Cascading in rapture and beating their breast
Against the stern granite with reckless unrest.

" Aye, let me forever stay thrilled by the shock
Of music-mad water quick kissing the rock,
Of dashing and plashing and throbbing its tune
In passionate pulses of ecstasy's swoon."

" Forever, forever," enamored she sighed,
" In waltz's weird measure, my being must glide,
Let motions of music, bewild'ring and dense
And tremor of touches bedazzle my sense."

Forever, forever, to senses of sound,
To shudders of sight, her being is bound,
Till all the red tides of poppies enflood
Her visions and dreams like rivers of blood.

Till all the wide waves of passion endrown
Her soul and her peace in tempest-tossed sound,
While all the wild wail of waters ensweeps
Her soul 'gainst the rocks of deep ocean deeps.

Forever, forever, sharp, sensuous sweets,
Sating and scathing,—too late—she entreats—
The peace and the calm of her soul lying still—
Murdered and buried by Passion's wild thrill !

NATURE'S JEWELS.

A JEWEL-CASE doth Nature hold,
     The emerald, chrysolite ;
The topaz for her days of gold,
     And jacinth for her night.

The chrysoprase and amethyst,
     And beryl for her skies ;
The jasper red and pearly mist
     To paint her fair sunrise.

SPRING.

An emerald—a verdant hint
     Of springtime air and grace
O'er earth and sky—the very tint
     Of woodlands in its face.

SUMMER.

And rich, in "sun-filled rapture," shone
     The topaz golden, bright—
Mid-summer sits upon her throne
     Above a sea of light.

AUTUMN.

Then shimmering down the chrysolite,—
 The woods a burnished green—
" The day all gold, all pearl the night,"
 While summer sleeps serene.

WINTER.

And last, a jacinth, purple skies
 Smile down on winter snows,
And deep, deep Night shuts fast her eyes
 On Nature in repose.

DEATH OF THE SUN.

I SAW him dying on his bed,
    A cloudy pillow for his head,
His coverlet of amber-red.

His curtains, canopies of light,
Enfringed with borders, beryl bright,
That gleamed against the walls of night.

I watched him sink—the sun grown old—
His touch did change each cloud to gold,
And, dying, warmed the twilight cold.

And where he might not reach, his smile
Lit all the sky for many a mile,
And let the world his light erewhile.

This sunlit life, magnanimous,
Reviving planets, generous,
Methinks 'tis glory to die thus—

Remembered in the days gone by,
Reflected in the sunset sky,
And mirrored in the moon on high !

LIFE

LIFE.

COME, enter our land of forests and flowers,
   Bound in by the skies and the trees,
The Island of Life — this earth-land of ours —
   Adrift on Eternity's seas.

See myriads of forms enthronging the Isle,
   Youth, Happiness, dreaming their dream,
Hark ! hear the sweet sound of music beguile
   Young Life fast fording the stream.

See pathways that ope to great mountain steeps,
   Smooth rivers that lead to the seas ;
See travelers, upon the deep ocean-deeps,
   Cross over to rest 'neath the trees.

Ye stars in the heavens, ye planets, look down,
   Reveal us the myst'ries of Time,
The shadowy past thy starlight did crown,
   Saw Life in her wonderful prime !

Ye infinite space, Eternity's reach,
   Pray, fathom Futurity's height,
Light-houses of Hope burn bright on the beach,
   Or ships may sink in the night.

Oh ! fathomless Life, so high and so deep,
   Half visible, hidden with God,
Descending thy depth or climbing thy steep,
   Weird windings will open untrod.

Uprise thee and brave, thy footsteps traverse
   The domain of Death's silent realm,
A Haven awaits in God's universe,
   Life-ship, with Faith at thy helm !

TWO VOICES.

TWO singing birds within her bosom dwelt.   At
    morn
  A little lark uprises to the sky and trills
His swelling note of ecstasy, deep, glad, free born;
    His heart breathed in his song, his bird-breast
        throbbing, thrills,
Till in sweet unison her bosom bounds
In joyous echoes to the matin sounds.

Of rosy dawns, of misty morning skies, he sings ;
  Of all the beauty hid in glistening dews ; of mirth
That bubbles up in fresh and varied founts, in springs
    Of sparkling thought whose bouyant bounty
        bathes the earth,
Till wood and sky unite and mate the beams
Of rising sun with dewdrop's rain-bow gleams.

But with the vesper chime of thought, the dusk of
    eve,
  The tender cooing of a dove in hymns of peace,
Uplifts her soul in holy harmony, doth weave
    A weird and wistful web around her heart, till
        cease

The soft vibrations of more sensuous sweets —
And all serene, her soul its silence meets.

And, mutely musing in the sanctum of this calm,
  The "virgin passion of her soul" steals forth
      and sings
The music of the moon, the song of stars, the balm
  Of tender thought borne upward on a dove's
      white wings,
Till soul and heaven meet and blend the glow
Of star-shine with the light upon her brow.

TWO PATHS.

TWO woodland paths, one free and wide,
  Where sunbeams loved to play,
Smiled on another at its side
  That in a shadow lay.

Two angels looked beneath the skies,
  One smiled across the light,
Two lives they blessed, but in one's eyes
  Tears dimmed the day to night.

Across the radiant life there shone
  The topaz, golden bright,
In " sun-filled rapture," diamond stone,
  A sheen of matchless light.

Till earthly pilgrims turned their feet
  Through it to heavenly heights,
Where chrysoprase and amethyst
  Reflect a thousand lights.

Across the next, a shade stole down
  And hung round heaven's shrine
A gem of stars to softer crown
  The moon-stone's solemn shine.

Till folded in the wings of Night
  Its chastened followers say :
" The darkness shows us worlds of light,
  We never saw by day ! "

At last, each life lost in one sun,
  " Where flame and azure meet,"
In heaven where day and night are one —
  An opal pure, complete.

TRANSFORMED.

FAIR and faultless as a statue, perfect in her outward mould,
Lived a maiden pure as marble, with a heart and
soul as cold.

Crowned with homage, many worshiped blindly at
her beauteous shrine,
But beneath the ivory image, not one glimpse of
life divine.

All in vain the blended magic of her choice charms
of art,
Vain and blank, her breathless beauty touched no
life and warmed no heart.

Till the Sculptor, with his chisel, cut and carved his
impress there,
Breathing from his living presence through the passage pulse of prayer.

Day by day, the marble mirrored new reflections of
his face,
Shone the very light of heaven in her benedictive
grace.

For each pang of pain she praised him, loved his
    chisel and his rod,
Transformed from the dust of beauty to the image
    of her God !

VIOLIN SONGS.

THE trembling, sobbing viol strings,
   Song-burdened, helpless little things—
One music touch and Silence sings.

The trembling breaks in music thrill,
The sobbing, one long glorious trill,
The silence in the heart's sweet still.

Sometimes a plaintive violin sings
As though the rustling of bright wings
Touched not, but trembled 'bove its strings;

As though some music in the air,
Some echo of a sweet despair,
Dropped in its heart and quivered there.

I listen to the violin song,
The pathos sweet, the passion strong,
The cadence tender, low and long,

And fancy that the bow that wrings
Its swelling heart and tender strings
Until soul music breaks and sings,

May be the arrow in disguise,
The gold-tipped dart, the strange surprise
That oped and closed some paradise.

And surer still that singing stream
That melts away in misty gleam
Is but the echo of some dream.

Ah! Silence, tell my sweet surmise,
This clear soul-song, the after rise
Of morning star in Easter skies!

MUSIC.

L IVING is music, if each beat of heart
     Be crystally pure and wedded with soul ;
If each note of action, with true steady start,
Blend chord and discord in one perfect whole.

SAINT CECILIA.

UNDERNEATH a western window, in the
hush of even shroud,
Ere the evening star rewakened on the bosom of
the cloud,

Sits a saint, in noiseless chamber, chaste as virgin
on her knees,
With her hands of ivory image on the organ's
ivory keys.

Stealing through the rich mosaic, in an arching,
bending bow,
Beams of beauty, blush and golden, crown her with
their sunset glow;

Touch her with a misty magic, heaven's glories
from afar,
Fold her in a fond reflection ; kiss upon her brow
their star.

Trembling there in blended brightness, on her fore-
head as a crown,
Sun and stars imprint their echoes, heaven's message wafted down.

Moved, but speechless in her rapture, seeing all
    Life's unseen goal,
With her lids low-drooped, but open wide the
    portais of her soul,

With the surge of silent music, hushed upon her
    parted lips,
Echoed through her breathing beauty, tingling
    nerves and finger-tips.

Ah! the living voice within her, overwhelming
    spoken word,
Speaks it meaning in the music of the echoed organ
    chord !

SATIRE OF THE DUCKS.

SOME silly ducks stepped from a pond
    And left their star foot-prints,
To counterfeit the stars beyond,
    T' eclipse the heavenly glints.

So we do paint us gilded wings,
    As children play their part,
Mistaking cheaper, finite things
    For poetry and art.

THE IDEAL.

SHE climbed the range of mountain heights,
    She left the Land of Real,
She bartered days for dreamy nights
    In search of Life's Ideal.

But misty visions met her view,
    Along this " Milky Way,"
And Fancy flickered for the True,
    Her footstep fell astray.

Till turning from Delusion's dome—
    Her journey not in vain—
She hears her Ideal's " Welcome Home "
    Within Life's lowly plain.

AMEN.

THERE was a little child whom God had made
     With beauty in her soul—and grave her face,
Cast in a perfect mould, but sad with shade
     Of loss and suffering—and quaint of grace
The shrinking, fragile form, till lone and shy,
She lived all silently with down-drooped eye.

She loved, with passion pent, but true and tense,
     All Beauty God had made—the sea, the sky,
And fancies colorful, but dim and dense
     The distance 'tween her grasp and ecstasy.
So feeling, loving all, but owning none,
Life's sweet interpreter yet lived on alone.

She sought the hidden paths, the silent ways,
     And let her inner soul grow pure and clear,
Interpreting Life's nights more than its days,
     Ere listening for some voice she might not hear—
Till tired of her tears, she kissed the rod,
Reflecting in her own the face of God !

THE SLEEPING ROCK.

UPON a craggy mountain side
  By lazy suns enclosed,
Through noiseless turns of time and tide,
 A rugged rock reposed,

Asleep, apart upon the crag,
 Aloof from life and toil,
To watch the wasting moments lag,
 The hopeful hours to spoil.

A Sculptor climbed the mountain height,
 Descried the sun-crowned stone,
Content to hide its beauty-light,
 To count its life its own.

And quick the iron struck the rock
 Like lightening's sudden start,
That crushed and crashed with subtle shock
 The granite's sleeping heart.

The powder thundered from its hold,
 The chisel cut and broke,
The Sculptor-hand with purpose bold
 Dealt hard each needed stroke.

Besplintered, broken, shattered, shorn,
    The chastened granite groaned,
Unsettled, rifted, left forlorn,
    In maddened memory moaned.

Rebellion rose, as head-long hurled,
    It fell from its high dome,
Its flag of hope forever furled
    Within its lowly home.

Past memories rack the rifted rock,
    Then rose the mist of pain,
Misunderstood each blasting shock —
    The chisel-touch in vain.

Till lo ! erect upon the sands,
    Within its alien home,
The Sculptor's perfect statue stands
    With heav'n-reaching dome.

The heav'n-light crowns its peerless spire,
    And given eyes to see,
Beholds its beauty, life entire,
    A stone to stand eternally.

SOUL.

SHE wove her life of myths and dreams,
Of fabrics made of rainbow gleams,
A woof of crimson, warp of gold,
Whose colors gay her stories told.

But no lips smiled and no hearts wept,
Within her life her soul still slept,
Her heart untouched, untaught its speech,
No other heart could touch or teach.

She sang of shells and ocean sprays,
Of purple nights and golden days,
The twinkling heart-beats of the stars,
But through her music blankness jars.

A motion moves her idle heart —
" My toils are dreams, my soul is art,
For one warm heart-beat, Ah!" she sighs,
" I'd give my gems of seas and skies!"

And Life comes close and hears her prayer,
And Death her heart embalms with care,
While to her lips their cup of pain
Is pressed for her young soul to drain.

Dark wine of life, it gurgles up,
The blood of hearts, red in her cup.
The dregs of death, the sighs of souls,
A tide of mingled sorrow rolls.

* * * *

From out the furnace of their pain
Her chastened lips would sing again,
Her harp is heart, her song is soul,
Her art is life and heaven its goal.

Her prism shines with tender light
Of human lives — their day and night —
And burning through her peerless art
The after-glow of radiant heart !

Her harmony is sympathy,
 Her key-note touch vibrates with love,
Her minor tones are melody,
 Her song the wide world's heart doth move.

"SHIPS THAT PASS IN THE NIGHT."

THE day is done, the ships passed on,
    A lonely soul at sea.
Its day has passed, its missing mast
    Retreats in memory.

But brave it wars, beneath the stars,
    The wrestling, seaward wave,
And hears again Life's "Might have been"
    Voiced in a watery grave.

Fair vessels sail the ocean deep,
    Ships passing in the night,
The lonely soul must wait and weep
    With friendly shores in sight.

Hope-laden ships alight with love,
    Pass by to Happy Land,
Faint voices echo, distant move
    Far down the far-off strand.

Ah ! soul at sea, Eternity
    Holds all thy "Might have been,"
The stars shine down on thee a crown,
    Sink, but to rise again !

OIL OF OLIVE, PEACE OF PALM.

SOMETIMES the surge of Life's unrest
   Sobs sharp, and sad, and sore oppressed,
Like ocean murmurs through my breast.

Swells strong and strange its seaward song
Of passion, pity, pain and wrong,
Till life is lone and loss is long.

Then 'bove the sun and shade of earth,
Beyond the sunset's golden girth,
Some better being finds its birth.

Its former Faith, its parent Pain,
Its tutor Trust, its self-hood slain,
And sweet its song as seraph's strain.

And blessedness and bliss embalm,
With oil of olive, peace of palm,
My restless soul in restful calm.

SUCCESS.

NOT he who boasts of bravest deeds,
      Of loudest vict'ry won ;
Nor he, who, wise in worldly creeds,
   Life's fairest feats has done.

But he who suffers pain and loss,
   Nor breaks his courage down,
He sits upon a throne, his cross
   Transfigured to a crown !

LOVE

LOVE.

AH ! wingèd winds and floating mists,
    And shining waves by rainbows kiss't,
Bear stilly down the lily stream
To twilight Isle where lovers dream.

Pause 'neath the shade of moss-hung trees,
Where bird-song trembles on the breeze,
Where pale, sweet moon, in virgin shroud,
Sleeps on a golden summer cloud ;

Where sunsets fade and leave the glint
Of rainbow 'cross the blue sky tint,
Where stealing through the clouds ajar,
The tender shine of '' Evening Star.''—

Here, on the Isle of Life, apart,
Two, hand in hand, each heart to heart,
Half-seen, through vistas lost in shade,
Love wanders down the starry glade ;

With silv'ry oar and golden barge,
Glides smoothly down the mossy marge,
Where skirts of light, and lily breath,
Bright belt the stream in flower wreath ;

Where faintest strains of music break
The solitude to gentle wake,
And all the senses sweetly move
To music, moonlit dreams and love !

THE WINDOW OF MY FANCY.

'TIS diamond paned and ruby stained,
    A mingle of mosaic ;
'Tis closed by light but opes by night,
    And shuts out all prosaic.

A blended dream of rainbow beam,
    A web of mystery ;
A woof of bright and warp of light,
    A roseate fantasy.

A net of hopes its shining opes,
    A timid ecstasy ;
A silver barge upon a marge
    Of sweet expectancy.

A minor chord, an echoed word,
    'Neath lover's canopy ;
A bolden dart, a golden heart
    Of Cupid's armory.

And, all in all, a sweet enthrall
    Of prodigality ;
A wasted maze of silver haze —
    And no reality.

LOVE'S RAINBOW.

HEAVEN bends her smiling skies
    For the lovers' canopies,
Hangs above her shining mark,
Promise to Love's drifting Ark.

Brilliant arch of prism lights,
Mingling suns and satellites ;
Gold and silver, pink and blue,
Shining sheen of rainbow hue.

Blue, for Love's sincerity;
Pink, for rosy ecstasy;
Silver, for the silver line
Turning every cloud to shine.

Gold, to gild the lovers' dreams,
Changing shadows into gleams;
Violet, to lift their eyes
To the fair, benignant skies.

LOVE'S AURORA.

YOUNG Life upon the threshold stands
    With laureled brow and flower-filled hands,
Success and hope, rich, starry gems,
Adorn her crown of diadems.

With light, free step, she lingers long,
Content to mingle with the throng,
To pluck the blossoms at her feet,
To place her urn 'neath fountains sweet.

But day grows long and night comes down,
And heavy grows the jeweled crown;
The blossoms droop, the laurels fade,
The sunshine pales to somber shade.

Her poor heart sighs, her spirit pines,
When lo! a presence radiant shines
That floods her gaze with trembling light,
Her sightless eyes with glorious sight.

A Light to tinge each mystery
With golden tint of ecstasy;
A Voice to fill the solitude
With music's sweetest interlude.

A Touch to thrill her senseless sense,
With strange vibrations, new, intense ;
A Vision, vivid, mingling sweet
Dismay, despair, delight complete.

A transient Heaven here on earth,
Where soul and being find their birth ;
Where time and life and memory move
In one eternal breath of love!

THE MESSAGE.

WHITE winged dove of poesy,
        Fly, a messenger for me,
To my love across the sea.

Ask eternal years to mark
Countless moments that embark
In Time's ever floating ark.

Bear so many thoughts for me,
Ceaseless as eternity,
Wingèd dove, across the sea.

Ask the diamond drops of dew,
To count the pearls—the varied hue—
Of their jewel-casket through.

Waft so many dreams for me,
Wingèd dove of constancy,
Kissed with seal of purity!

ON THE WINGS OF LOVE.

Suggested by Heine's "Auf Flugeln des Gesanges."

ON the wings of love, heart's dearest, where
    all mystery is shrined,
To the sanctum of soul's silence, where sweet
    secrets are divined.

To the land of golden fancies, Nature's beauties,
    Art and Love,
Where the bow of Dreamland dances from a starry
    arc above.

Thence I bear thee to a woodland, verdant bloom-
    ing to the sky,
Waiting stilly with the blossoms for thy footsteps
    coming nigh.

Where the peeping blue-orbed violets mutely meet
    our gaze of love,
Where the whispering wild blush roses through
    the forest shadows rove.

Where the laughing water waltzes with coquettish
    sprays of light,
O'er a silv'ry, rocky pavement, far into the moon-
    lit night.

There, beneath the bending willows, venturing to
    the water's edge,
Whisper to the night our secret, to your heart my
    loving pledge !

WAITING.

I NEVER saw his face,
   The face of smiling Love,
Yet, sure am I some day he'll come
   And all my being move.

I never felt the thrill
   Of lover's temp'rament,
Yet some strange day, my heart may fill
   With sweet bewilderment.

I never heard the strain
   Of his great rhapsody,
Yet, I am sure Love will explain
   To me his mystery.

My years have come and gone,
   Yet, I am sure 'tis given
The waiting heart to find its own—
   If not on earth—in heaven!

FOUR-LEAVED CLOVER.

"TWO, three, four," she counts them over,
    Love's quatrain of four-leaved clover.
Wears the verdant, velvet petals
Near her heart—her sweet requitals.

"Two, three, four, true, he does love me,
Sure as stars that shine above me—"
Ah! the melting, madd'ning vision
Of her happy heart elysian!

Footsteps following close behind her,
He, in search of sweet reminder
Of her vanished face and graces—
Looks in woodland's shady places.

Till he, too, enraptured lover,
Plucks a velvet four-leaved clover,
"Two, three, four,—true, she will love me,
Sure as stars that shine above me!"

Faster falls his footstep, fleeter
Than the steps of Signiorita,
And his eyes of vivid vision,
See across the fields elysian.

"Two, three, four," their songs united,
Two shy hearts the clover plighted,
Since their badges and their songs
Prove that each to each belongs—

And just there in "Fields Elysian,"
Ceremonies in derision,
Four-leafed clover, four lips rosy
Blend, a single clover-posy!

TWO VERSIONS.

THE light of dreams shines in her eyes—
   Her heart perplexed 'tween smiles and
  sighs
    And aspirations deep.
" Where Muses walk," she quotes him low,
And puts a pause to passion's vow,
    " There, lovers needs must creep."

The light of hope shines in his face,
As in her lines his heart may trace
    Another meaning deep.
" Ah! pretty maid, his lips afrown,
Methinks your book is upside-down,
    Pray, take another peep."

The roses paint her cheek and brow,
While he, in turn, quotes to her now,
    His voice impassioned deep—
" Where lovers walk," his love is bliss—
Her cheek and lips blush with his kiss—
    " Why, Muses needs must creep !"

FROM HEART TO SOUL.

CLOSE beside a grave, a maiden lingers while
    the shadow's gloom,
Lays her cherished hopes and passions in a cold
    and silent tomb.

Change has robbed her of her idol, of her golden
    dream of love,
Hushed the incry of her fancies, startled from its
    rest her dove.

Once, she owned a heart of treasures, Love's soft
    sunshine 'round her hair
Hung in halo crowns of glory, kissed her lips and
    bosom fair.

Suddenly a Sculptor chiseled young Life's budding,
    blushing bloom
From the flushing flesh to marble, hid her heart
    within a tomb.

Through the vista of the silence, like lost chords
    of Love forlorn,
Wistfully she hears the music of her happy yester-
    morn.

As a statue 'neath the arches of the heaven's
    tender blue,
Stands this modest maiden marble, pale and pure
    in pallid hue.

Grief has touched, with chastened chisel, her up-
    lifted arms and face,
Kissed each line and curve of beauty with pure
    lips of spirit grace.

Hope shines through the earthly shadows, hope
    transmutes her pain to peace,
Resurrected from the ashes of her heart, her soul's
    release !

THE CASTLE OF CLOUDS.

I BUILT a castle in the clouds,
   With weird and misty dome,
A sepulchre of sacred shrouds
   For hopes without a home.

For hearts that dreamed their dreams in vain,
   For chords of music lost,
For cadences of patient pain,
   Fair visions ne'er recross't.

For ships that see their setting sun
   Sink ere they reach their shore,
For songs that cease when scarce begun,
   For lives that sing no more.

For love whose wings have touched the gate
   Of highest paradise
To find it closed, its coming late,—
   For all lost memories.

Within this temple in the clouds,
   Lost treasures of the heart
Lie smiling, in their virgin shrouds,
   From all the world apart.

Shine softly suns above the place,
   Transforming dome and spire,
And lorn Dian with vigil face
   Touch with thy holy fire

The turrets of this still domain,
   Till Time shall fade away,
Till all the lost shall rise again
   On Resurrection Day.

LOVE'S RETROSPECT.

WHEN the dying day is done,
    In the wane of setting sun,
Sitteth one in twilight dun,
Singing sadly, softly, low,
Of Life's sunset's fading glow
In Love's tender Long Ago.

When the reapers garner sheaves,
When the golden autumn trees
Flame and drop their falling leaves,
Sings again the same refrain,
Through a silver mist of pain,
Of fading leaf and sobbing rain.

Watching still the closing year
With the night-winds wailing drear,
And the moonlight cold and clear,
Sings, once more, the echoed chime
Borne along the tide of Time
Of eternal love sublime.

LOVE'S VESPER.

ABOVE the Isle of Love, at last,
    When starry dawns and suns have passed,
Love's vesper-star—soft after-glow—
Breaks on the waiting hearts below.

Its shine is tender, clear and calm
With less of thrill but more of balm,
Serene reflection in each heart
Of Life and Love ere they must part.

Love purified and chastened sweet
To purest gold through furnace heat;
Love glorified with holy fire,
The music of celestial choir.

No passion-gust to dim or mar
The spirit light of vesper-star;
No storm-tossed hopes to break the poise
Of souls attuned to sacred joys.

Shine soft and still, pale star of Age,
Best benedictions on Love's page,
And beckon to thy sky-lit dome—
While heart's sweet mem'ries gather home !

HEAVEN.

HEAVEN.

COME, sing of a land—the "Land of the
  Sky—"
  With only a River between
To hide the fair haze, the sweet mystery
  Of heaven and glory from men.

No vision or trance—Reality shines,
  Surpassing the glory of star,
A halo of gems above the gold lines
  That stream from the Gates swung ajar.

Neath arches of light, the mazes and mist
  Blend beryl and jacinth and gold,
Where sapphire and pearl and pure amethyst
  Interpret all Beauty untold.

Deep vistas of shade, enfringing the aisle
  Of rivers that lead to the throne,
Where Silence and Awe meet—waiting God's smile
  That welcomes to heaven His own.

Soft echoes of harp trill trembles of peace,
  Till Silence and Music are one,
While spirits, transformed in blessed release,
  Bright image His glorious Son!

Sweet Spirit of Song, thy bosom doth keep
  All music and myst'ry and bliss;
All heaven transport in one thrilling sweep,
  All silence in one holy kiss.

Touch tenderly harps, while ecstasy shines
  Its radiance on flowers and streams,
Till vividly clear in gold, shining lines
  Are written lost visions and dreams.

Fair City of Light, of cedar and palm,
  There, Beauty and Love find their goal ;
There, clear, cooling springs and breezes of balm
  Await in the Home of the Soul!

MY SONG.

LORD, speak Thy message to my soul and let
me sing
    A song for Thee;
My life is poor and blank, a paltry, perished thing,
    O, live in me.

I have no human gifts, no earthly hopes of joy,
    Accept me Lord;
Bequeath this gift of song as means in Thine em-
ploy
    To speak Thy word.

And, if in school of grief, Thou deem it wise to
train
    My voice for Thee,
Through losses and defeat and passages of pain,
    There, Lord, lead me.

Through climbing mounts of toil with just enough
of hope
    To bid me rise,
Through narrow valley shades, just dim enough to
ope
    The starry skies ;

Through pastures green, or barren field, my soul
    to teach
        Thy training skill,
Through loss or gain—the valley depth, or moun-
    tain reach,
        O, work Thy will!

And then, from all my gleanings, Lord, I'd yield
    to Thee
        One chastened word,
Oh, let it be from earth-stain washed, from dross
    all free,
        Thy flaming sword

To probe the hearts of flesh, to touch, to burn with
    breath
        Of holy fire,
To lift immortal souls thro' grave of mortal death
        To life entire!

THE INNER ROBE.

IT speaks of Thee, Thy cleansing power,
    Thy righteousness,
This robe—the Christian's heavenly dower,
    His blessedness.

Lord, shield it from all earthly taint,
    Enveil me o'er,
Enfold me in Thy strong restraint,
    Behind, before.

And lead me in the shining lines
    Of purity,
In path that sweetens and refines
    My chastity.

Let naught of look or tone impart
    A sordid trace,
No barrier between my heart
    And Thy fair face.

Naught that I read, or think, or glean
    In Beauty, Art;
May Thy white Image ever screen
    The hidden part.

Oft I must walk 'mid earthly glare,
    Lend me Thine eyes
To see whatever things are fair
    In human guise.

Then bid me know the chaff from wheat—
    Yet, not to know—
To keep my robe as fresh and sweet
    As "unsunned snow."

ENOCH.

GOD made a life with soul too high
    For this poor earth to satisfy,
A heart with yearnings too intense
To fill its depths with earth's pretence.

The love of friends—aye, kindred seemed
But shadow-types of all he dreamed,
He sought a silent path and trod
A life apart, alone with God.

He lives, yet dwells not on this earth,
He claims his heritance and birth,
His Home beyond Death's bed of sod,
This dual life that walked with God.

THE VALLEY OF BACA.

DARK valley-depth, still, stagnant stream,
  With weeping-willow trees,
Weird solitude and shadow-dream
  That haunt like moaning seas.

Hush, hear the voice of Sorrow speak,
  The silent voice of God,
Each subtle sound and semblance seek,
  Lean on the chastening rod.

Lo, clear well-springs in desert place—
  Abloom the ashen dell—
The valley wears a smiling face,
  My soul, "make it a well."

GOD IN NATURE.

I GAZED upon a lofty mount,
   The stones that stud its pages,
The time-worn strata that recount
   Its dynasties for ages,—
When spoke a voice to Nature known,
   Despite the creed of sages,
"Geology, thy corner-stone,
   Itself, the 'Rock of Ages.'"

I looked across the blooming wold
   Of brightly waving posies,
And learned the flower-secrets told
   By golden-hearted roses—
While echoed in my soul, half hushed,
   This voice of melody,
"Within the 'Rose of Sharon,' blushed
   The bloom of Botany."

Beneath the heaven's starry scroll,
   I watched the stars' slow passage,
Their bright handwriting on the wall,
   Their silent, heavenly message;

" Astronomy, pale Venus, Mars,
　　Your brightest diadem
Encrowns all satellites and stars—
　　' The Star of Bethlehem.' "

THROUGH DEATH TO LIFE.

AN angel wrestled with my heart,
　　He claimed all human bliss,
I suffered—died—and watched depart
The rosy touch of Love and Art,
　　All hopes poor earthlings miss !

And, then, I paused in wonder start,
　　No will I'd had but mine,
Till now I prayed with deepest heart,
Lord, here am I, alone, apart,
　　No more mine own, but Thine.

"My child," the Voice was low and sweet,
　　"Now is all fulness thine,
Lie still and lowly at my feet,
Until the workmanship's complete
　　And all thy will is Mine."

He oped my eyes, and then I saw
　　A glorious Hope and Love
Transformed in Him, unflecked with flaw ;
My buried life, in upraised awe,
　　Rose as a wingèd dove.

And for the loss of earth He gave
  The recompense of Heaven ;
For human hope, His hope ; for grave,
Eternal life—Himself to save
  When self from self was riven !

I DREAMED AND SAW AN ANGEL MAKING CROWNS.

I DREAMED and saw an angel making crowns—
   An arc of gold beset with gems—
And weaving fair and bright seraphic gowns,
   All glistening with diadems.

Some saintly soul to wear the robe, some brow
   To claim the priceless, star-gemmed crown.
But, angel, pause and tell me where and how
   The glory comes for gem and gown.

"These robes," she said, "are Christ's own
     righteousness—
   Made of the ransom He provides,
But, these fair diadems," with sweeter stress,
   She speaks, while pointing 'neath the skies,

"These diadems, these jewel-jets are made,
   Not from the gloss of angel's wing,
But from the smile of souls amid earth's shade—
   From souls they win—from gifts they bring.

These little gems you see in clustered light,
    That shine as dew-drops 'gainst the glow,
Are tears of pain and penitence through night
    Of wrestling souls with sin and woe.

" Some jewels shine for other souls they've won,
    A myriad arc of smiles and tears,
But, 'bove the starry-stones, the summit's sun—
    The fairest gem this image wears,

" The image of a smile caught from a soul
    Passed under Pain's most chastening rod,
When all its utmost done and missed its goal,
    It lifts its face and smiles toward God ! "

COMMUNION.

ON the wings of prayer, departed, where all
    sanctity doth bloom,
To the silence of His Presence, when the shades of
    evening gloom ;

'Neath the tender twilight heavens where the stars
    are shining down
On us, meeting in communion, all their chastened
    halo crown ;

There, I find thee in this sanctum, set apart for
    kindred hearts,
Where the music-voice of heaven all its restfulness
    imparts ;

Where the presence of His Spirit wraps our spirits
    twain in one,
Where His Love and Light and Glory meet in
    one effulgent sun ;

Where all pain and grief transmuted, where all loss
    is counted gain,
Where discordant harps are softened to submis-
    sion's sweetest strain ;

There, in spirit thought communing of the holy joys
    above,
Triune souls, we with the Saviour, in one will, one
    life and love !

RECOMPENSE.

THE caterpillar murmurs much
    When first he feels the forming touch
That would transform the clumsy thing,
A butterfly with gilded wing.

So our hearts do sigh and break
If God our human angels take,
In wise and loving discipline,
To bring the great archangels in !

"SELAH."

THE Psalmist harped of music, love,
　　And sang of passions sad and sharp,
But grandest strains in silence move
　　Beneath the "Selah of his harp."

The Poet pours his prayer of song
　　In thrilling voice, divinely fair,
But noblest throbs of thought belong
　　Beneath the Selah of his prayer.

Great Nature speaks her mirth and pain
In joyous breeze and sobbing rain,
Her highest voices breathe and brood
Within the Selah of her mood.

And may not God in solemn still
　　Breathe tenderly in awe-hushed chords,
Revealing silently His Will
　　Beneath the Selah of His Words?

LONGING.

MY loving heart craves deepest love,
  My spirit seeks to rise,
My better self, my soul would move
  To love that satisfies.

No human bliss, no tender tie,
  No idol to bedim
The shining peace and unity
  My soul would find in Him.

So take me, Lord, and make me Thine,
  And let me reach in Thee,
The glory of a love divine,
  Enough of joy for me.

SATISFIED.

TO know and see Thee as Thou art,
   Thy glory and Thy grace,
To feel Thee near me, heart to heart,
   To see Thee face to face.

To feel Thy fulness in my soul,
   The Spirit's holy thrill,
The anchor of Thy safe control,
   The sweetness of Thy will.

To know the riches of Thy love,
   The satisfying glow,
No other joys my heart so move,
   No higher good to know !

THE RIVER OF HIS PEACE.

ON-ROLLING tide of Promises,
   Smooth-shining stream serene,
Mute in thy smiling mysteries,
   God's Image in thy sheen.

There let me float in restfulness,
   My soul in sweet release,
Stayed on His loving mindfulness,
   Lost in His " perfect peace."

No wrestling wave, no tempest sound,
   No storm-tossed, sobbing noise,
No restless hopes of hearts earth-bound,
   To mar the music poise.

Float on my soul, attuned, at rest,
   Where peace and calm ne'er cease,
Serene and pillowed on the breast
   Of God's unchanging Peace.

CROWNED.

ESTRANGED, apart, a stranger-guest,
    Of lowly birth,
Misunderstood, unknown, unblest,
    A soul on earth—
With heartaches sore, with missing links
    From out Life's chain,
Of many bitter cups he drinks,
    Of loss and pain.

Till heaven smiles and bids him rise
    On spirit wing—
Congenial souls in Paradise
    His praises sing—
For loneliness, for dearth, for loss,
    They, stooping down,
Receive him *lowest* at the cross
    To *highest* crown !

www.ingramcontent.com/pod-product-compliance
Lightning Source LLC
Chambersburg PA
CBHW030551270326
41927CB00008B/1595